I0480529

INTERNET MARKETING METRICS

The 8 Most Important Metrics to Track for Ensuring Success of eCommerce Websites

Charles Abeghe

DISCLAIMER

This e-book has been written for information purposes only. Every effort has been made to make this eBook as complete and accurate as possible. However, there may be mistakes in typography or content. Also, this e-book provides information only up to the publishing date. Therefore, this eBook should be used as a guide - not as the ultimate source.

The purpose of this eBook is to educate. The author and the publisher do not warrant that the information contained in this e-book is fully complete and shall not be responsible for any errors or omissions. The author and publisher shall have neither liability nor responsibility to any person or entity with respect to any loss or damage caused or alleged to be caused directly or indirectly by this e-book.

Charles Abeghe Charene

Holdings Inc,

#161, 234-5149 Country Hills Blvd NW, Calgary, AB T3A 5K8, Canada

www.chareneinc.com

TABLE OF CONTENTS

INTRODUCTION

They say that 'that which is measured, grows'. That is to say that the simple act of measuring some metric or other can be enough to help that metric improve. This is true for weight loss, where simply weighing yourself regularly can help the pounds fall off and of course it is true of digital marketing.

If you are not measuring the progress of your website or the growth, then there is no way for you to apply the scientific method to ensure that it *continues* on an upward trajectory. Without measuring, you have no way of knowing what's working and what isn't and you are essentially flying blind!

But measuring the success of a website is something that requires a certain science in itself. What precisely should you be measuring? What are the most important metrics? And how do these numbers work together to provide a detailed understanding of your traffic and your success? This guide will attempt to answer all those questions and more by focusing on the 8 most
important metrics you need to be tracking!

1. TRACK VISITS

The first thing to look at is the number of visits you are getting to your website. This metric in itself is not necessarily all that useful, seeing as it doesn't necessarily provide much information regarding the type of person visiting your site, the way they're engaging with your content or anything else.

What's more, is that most websites will not see a visit as the 'end goal'. If you are intending on building brand awareness, engagement and following, then you will need to reduce your bounce rate (see below). If you are trying to make money, then your 'goal' will be to increase your AdSense revenue, or to make more sales of your products. Visits in itself is really just an aside!

Despite this though, you need to know your visits in order to make sense of all the other data that you're getting. You need to know your visits so that you can know what *percentage* of those visitors are buying from you and thereby calculate your conversion rate.
Your visits tell you how many people you have to work with and they let you formulate a strategy on that basis.

And if your main income comes from AdSense *impressions* (rather than clicks), then there is a very good chance that your number of visits is going to correlate pretty much directly with your overall revenue.

When looking at this metric though, it's important to recognize the subtle distinctions between the different kinds of 'hits' and 'visits'.

For example, you have both 'visits' and 'unique visits'. In many ways, the latter is actually more useful as this uses cookies stored on your visitors' computers in order to identify repeat visitors. So if you have one mega fan who visits your website 20 times a day, then your 'unique visits' metric will help you to compensate for that and give you a more useful number that is a better reflection of your site's popularity.

Another thing to consider is the difference between 'hits' and 'visits'. Hits are different from visits because they actually represent every single demand placed on your servers. This means each new visit to your site but it also means image that gets downloaded and might also include 'bots' (scripts that work for search engines and other sites as a way of indexing the content on your site).

This means that if someone were to link directly to one of your images and embed it on your page (which isn't the done thing but it does happen!), then you would see a massive increase in your hits that wouldn't necessarily tell you anything about how many people were actually *reading* your content.

So at the very least, you should look at visits rather than hits. And most likely you are going to want to look at your *unique* visits more than that. And even then, this metric is going to be most useful when used in conjunction with others. Nevertheless, this is your starting point and it is the first metric you need to track. It is the broadest and most general descriptor of your overall success and is definitely a useful number to watch.

Note: This is a good time for us to point out that none of these metrics is infallible and it is certainly possible to 'fool' the reports. For example, if someone is using private browsing on their computer, then they won't be storing cookies and that means that they may be counted as a new visitor (although normally the IP address is also taken into account). If a user has multiple computers more likely, then this too can also upset your statistics.

How to Increase Your Visits

So how do you go about increasing your page visits? The first thing you are doing correctly is monitoring them and seeing how they increase, as this way you can now try to make changes and see how your site improves or does n't. This will then let you know what's working, what you need to change and more.

There are numerous different ways to increase page views and basically the answer here is: marketing. These days, that can include:

- SEO
- Social media marketing

- Content marketing
- Advertising

The key is to create a synergy between all these things and have a strong brand that drives through all of them. Content is very much the key as unless you're a big, well-recognized online store, this is what is going to give people a *reason* to come to your website and it is what Google is going to be able to index and use to decide where you should appear on the SERPs (Search Engine Results Page). Content builds trust and engagement and encourages your visitors to share your site on social media and it gives *you* something of value to offer on social media too.

From there, you can also focus on building inbound links to your site from reputable and trusted domains, as well as using influencer marketing by teaming up with other brands and site owners to increase your exposure.

The last element – advertising – of course means spending money on a CPC (cost-per-click) ad campaign, a banner or perhaps a video ad. This will bring its own set of metrics, which is something we'll be looking at more further into this post.

2. BOUNCE RATE

Your bounce rate tells you what proportion of your traffic lands on your site and then immediately leaves. This is a bounce and it basically means that although you have a visit, you aren't engaging with that visitor and they aren't stopping to read what you've created.

This is a good example of why visits don't tell the whole story. If you have 1,000 daily visits with a 99% bounce rate, then that means that only 10 people are actually sticking around to read your site!

But bear in mind that a bounce rate still doesn't tell the *whole* story. That's because a bounce rate isn't based on the amount of time they spend on your site but rather their interaction. So someone might bounce from your site after spending a while there – and this simply means that they didn't click to read any of your other pages.

So even if you have a bounce rate at about 60%, that doesn't necessarily mean that visitors aren't reading your site – they may be reading the page but simply not feeling the need to read further. If your 'site' is a one page sales script, then this won't necessarily be a bad thing!

A good bounce rate is generally thought to be anything from 26%- 60% and you can consider anything under 30% to be very much in the 'outstanding' category. Being around 40% is very average and shouldn't be a cause for concern. If you're about 55%, then you're getting into the higher portion but again, this is only a cause for concern depending on the type of site that you are running.

Finally, if you have a bounce rate over 70%, then that is considered poor/disappointing regardless of the nature of your website or blog.

As a general rule, your bounce rate is arguably more important than your visits because it tells you about engagement and what percentage of your traffic is likely to come back, is likely to buy from you and is likely to become a 'fan'.

A similar metric to this is your 'average time on site'. This is similar to a bounce rate but can potentially be even *more* brutal, as it tells you how many of your visitors visited your site, spent a few seconds on your page and then left immediately!

The average time on site metric is a very useful one for illustrating engagement too but as with bounce rates, it's important not to get too worried if your metric doesn't look good. The thing to remember is that 55% of visitors will spend fewer than 15 seconds on your website regardless of the content.

You could write an entire article about why this is. Suffice to say that as a species, we humans are becoming more impulsive and more impatient. We always feel busy, we always feel rushed for time and we rarely feel that we have the time to stop and smell the roses – let alone stop and read a website that we find generally interesting!

How to Shrink Your Bounce Rates

The question you really need to be asking yourself, is how you can get your bounce rates lower and your time on site higher.

There are many different factors that play a role here. One such factor is the design of your website and as in real life, first-impressions are incredibly important here! If someone visits your website and they feel that it isn't particularly attractive or well designed, then this might be enough to cause them to immediately turn and leave!

The colors you use can have a big influence here and it's worth looking into things like color psychology. For instance, did you know that the color red tends to make people leave faster? Blue and other 'cool colors' meanwhile have a calming effect and lead to visitors spending longer on a page as a result.

Another very important thing to look at with regards to your bounce rates is your page load times. Countless studies and reports confirm that this is a huge influencing factor that can be devastating for your site's performance. If your visitors have to wait even a few seconds for your page to load, they will very often get bored and turn away. Make sure that you use as many speed optimization tricks as you possibly can to help your site appear as soon as the visitor has typed the address into their URL bar and hit 'enter'. Reduce the number of large images, use AJAX scripts to change the order of loading elements and make sure that you're on a good hosting package.

Always avoid large blocks of text too. Remember what we just said: people are always in a hurry. They don't have time to wait for your site to load but they *also* don't have time to read through massive swathes of information. You can combat this issue by breaking up your text into smaller, more spread-out paragraphs and by using lots of headings. Ideally, your headings should contain a lot of the information in your site so that someone would be able to skim through your site *only* reading the headings and still get a complete picture of what it is you want to say.

From there, the key is then to *keep checking back* to see how your changes are actually affecting your website. This is the entire point of using metrics in the first place – as now by checking back you'll able to see which of your changes has helped and which has made no difference. Do more of the former and less of the latter!

3.   PAGE VIEWS AND AVERAGE PAGE VIEWS PER VISIT

Your page views is a metric that sites somewhere snuggly between your views and your hits. This basically tells you how many individual pages have been viewed, regardless of who viewed them or how many times. Thus it might also be referred to as impressions.

Your page views are important in their own way because they tell you how many times the content on your site is being loaded up. And if you have a lot of CPM ads (pay cost per impression), then that tells you how much you're going to earn from them. It's also useful to consider aspects like your unique visits vs page views when you look at factors like conversion rates (below). This is useful because each new page view can be considered a new chance for you to impress your visitors.

This metric is closely related to another very useful one: that being the average page views per visit. This is similar to your bounce rate but provides a little more in-depth data that shows you how many different pages your visitor looked around on your site. This is a very useful thing to know because it can tell you whether you are being successful in getting your visitors to not only interact with your site but also to keep reading.

If you think of your visitors in terms of leads, then the visitors who read the most pages on your site are the most engaged with your brand and are thus the 'warmest leads'. The more page views you get from each visitor, the more likely it is that they will eventually buy when they see your product.

Another related metric/term that you should keep an eye on is your average cost per page view. This tells you how much you are paying to get each hit on your page. If you aren't doing any paid marketing, then of course this will likely be a very small number (the only cost being your hosting). But if you are spending money on AdWords and other things, then this is a useful way to look at your expenses.

Now this is a metric that won't be readily available in most dashboards. But the thing to keep in mind is that most of the *most valuable* metric in internet marketing aren't; you need to calculate them yourself!

To work this one out, all you need to do is take the average spend on your website and then divide it by the number of page views.
Don't forget to include all your other costs too in order to make this data as accurate as possible.

How to Increase Your Page Views

How do you increase your page views?

Other than by marketing your site to increase visits, the other thing you need to do is to keep your visitors on your page and to keep them reading. Remember how we said that content was the key to SEO and to social media marketing? Well, it's also the key to engagement. This is why it's not enough for you to simply create a *lot* of content – you also need to make sure that your content is top quality and is unique, interesting and generally the sort of thing people actually want to read and stick around for.

You can also use plugins and other techniques to try and encourage people to stick around and go deeper down your rabbit hole. For example, WordPress plugins showing 'related posts' can be very helpful in this regard because they suggest similar content based on what the visitor is already enjoying.

Another useful strategy is to make multi-part articles. This is why you will often see posts split into lots of pages: it increases the page views and thereby increases the impressions for adverts that you are earning from!

Note that advertising itself is actually *bad* for your page views. Why? Because when someone clicks on an advert, they invariably get taken away from your site! Even if the new page opens up in another window or tab, that can still be enough to break the engagement. This is why you shouldn't put AdSense on a sales page!

4. TRACK REFERRERS

Not all of the data you'll find in your Analytics or WordPress dashboards is going to be quantitative – some of it will be qualitative, meaning that it doesn't show numbers but rather details.

And the most important of that qualitative data is the referrer. Your referrer section shows you *where* your traffic is coming from. Are more of your visits coming from Google for instance? Or are they coming from your Facebook page?

This is very important for countless reasons. For starters, this lets you see which of your marketing efforts are paying off and which money is well spent – which is something that looking at your profits can't necessarily tell you. If you spend money on an SEO service for example and your profits don't go up, you might be tempted to think the company isn't doing its job. But if you look closer and realize that your referrers from Google have gone up massively, then that might tell you that the problem isn't with the SEO company but with your bounce rates, or your product.

Likewise, you can look at your referrers as a way to see what *kind* of person is coming to your site. If you have a product aimed at martial artists and all your traffic is coming from a martial arts forum then this tells you a few things. A) That forum is a good source for future links, b) you should look into getting more links from similar sites and c) you might want to consider making a product for martial artists.

Pay careful attention to your referrers so that you can improve all the other metric and so that you can spot anomalies that could upset your data!

5. TRACK CONVERSION RATES

Your conversion rate tells you how many of your visitors are 'converting' in the way that you want them to. In most cases, that is going to mean that they are buying a product from you – but it could also mean that they're signing up to a mailing list or even that they're clicking on an advert on your website. This is the point at which your site has achieved its end goal.

The way you track conversion rates is a little different, seeing as this is a flexible term that can mean very different things depending on the nature of your website and your business. The way you are normally going to do this, is by using 'goals'. Goal tracking basically means that you place a script on your 'goal page' and this then leaves a cookie on the browsers of your visitors. That goal page will likely be the 'Thank you for subscribing' page, or perhaps your order confirmation page. You know that once a visitor reaches this page, they will have to have converted.

In turn, that also means that you can now track their trajectory through your website and you can see what proportion of your visitors make it to that page.

Tracking conversion rates is incredibly important for the majority of online businesses because this is what is going to have the biggest impact on your 'bottom line'. A lot of people believe that they need to focus on increasing their views and engagement but if you are looking at your website from a purely business perspective, then conversion rates are really all that matter.

How do you know if your advertising expenses were a good investment? Only by tracking your goals and looking at your conversion rates.

And likewise, tracking your conversion rates is the only way that you get more people to buy your products in a systematic way. As with the previous metrics we've looked at, once you *know* your numbers in this area, you can then make changes to try and improve them and track whether or not your changes are actually making a positive impact.

How to Improve Your Conversion Rates

The great thing about your conversion rates is that you have full control over all of the factors influencing them.

When you're looking at your visits for example, this is partly going to be dictated by your search ranking. While you can do everything you can do to improve your search ranking, the final decision ultimately lies with Google. The algorithm they use is a secret and thus no guarantees can be made. Sometimes you will see spikes or troughs in your number of views, hits or page views and be completely unable to do anything about it.

Your conversion rates might change inexplicably too and they might seem mysterious sometimes. But you still control all the factors – from your product, to the price, to the sales script, to the site design. And that means you can keep tweaking until you get the precise result you're looking for.

And there's a great strategy you can use to accomplish this, called 'A/B Testing' or 'Split Testing'. Here, you essentially create two identical versions of your website with just one slight change and then you compare them to each other, while paying close attention to the metric.

So for example, if your conversion rates aren't quite as high as you'd like them to be and you blame your ugly header font, then you can try to make two identical versions of your site with only the heading being different. You'll then send a portion of your visitors to the new version with the new header and you'll be able to compare the conversion rates. If the new site is making far more sales from the same number of visitors, then you can adopt that new change across all your sites. If it isn't, you just reject the changes!

Conversion Rates Vs Views

A relatively new term in the world of marketing, sales and persuasion is something called 'pre-suasion'.

The general idea behind this term, is to get the customer *ready* to want to buy from you. The argument is that people are much more likely to buy at certain times and especially if you have made the effort to get them in the mood for buying first. People are more likely to buy in the evening for example because when we're tired, we become more impulsive and more emotional.

What's more though, is that people are more likely to buy from you when they have gotten to know your brand and when they are convinced that you know what you're talking about. The same logic applies to dating – you're more likely to get a girl/guy's number if you have spent longer chatting to them and showing them that you're fun to hang out with!

So one of the best ways to improve your conversion rates is to show the *right kind of person* your sales page. You can do this by showing visitors your sales page only after they have racked up a number of page views for example, or by using strategies like remarketing.

Of course targeting is also important – and that means showing your site to the correct demographics. Are more of your buyers young men? Then target young men with your advertising and

SEO! Find out what young men want to read and put *that* content on your website!

Other Factors

Of course there are also a ton of other factors influencing your conversion rates. Perhaps the biggest of these is your sales copy. The more persuasive you are in selling the positive aspects of your product and the better you are at applying sales pressure (i.e. showing your buyers that the product is limited in supply etc.). These are all things you can experiment with.

Obvious the product is also a VERY big factor and that means the desirability of said product, the target demographic and the price. These are factors you can play with, especially once you know the cost of your page views.

6. RATE OF RETURN VISITORS

Rate of Return Visitors is another metric that will give you more insight regarding the actual engagement you're enjoying on your website. As the name rather suggests, this will tell you how much of your traffic is generated by visitors who keep coming back to your site.

This metric is harder to track in a true manner because people will change computers and cookies over time. However, by looking at IPs and tracking how many of those are changing over time, you can get a good estimate of how many of your visitors have been fans for a long time – but this will be slightly skewed by your number of new users. Using something like a user login can help you to improve the accuracy of this metric somewhat depending on the tools you use, as this way users with new computers can log in using their old accounts and thereby identify themselves.

But in this case, a rough estimate is good enough for your purposes. The aim is just to get a rough percentage of how much of your traffic is new traffic. And this is very important, seeing as it can tell you a lot about the nature of your visits.

For example, if you have a lot of visits, then you might think that this means you have a very successful marketing campaign. But then if you take a closer look and realise that the vast majority of those visits are from people who check your site once a week… suddenly you realize that your engagement is *great* but your marketing is not so hot. This illustrates a very obvious area for improvement.

Or what about sites with excellent rates of return visitors but terrible conversions? This is interesting because you would expect a site with high levels of conversions and clear *fans* to get a lot of sales and a lot of subscribers. If that's not what you're seeing, then it could suggest that the product is not very enticing for your visitors, it could suggest that you are using too much of a 'soft sell approach' or it could mean that you need to fix the sales copy on that page.

How to Improve Your Rate of Return Visitors

Of course this is again an area where it is very important to make sure your site is *great* and that the content is the writing of thing that keeps bringing your visitors back.

But at the same time, you can also use a number of other tricks to encourage regular visits. One example is to create multi-part articles that show up once a week. Likewise, you can also increase your return visitors by talking about upcoming posts and events that will get your readers exciting.

Perhaps the single most important thing though is to make sure you are consistent. This means you should post your new content on a consistent basis but it also means you need to stick to one topic and one tone. People tend to subscribe to sites or to bookmark them because they want a regular dose of information or entertainment. If they keep checking back and there's no new content, then you might lose a follower.

Social media and email marketing are also very useful for bringing people back to your site repeatedly, as this way you can remind people that your brand exists and encourage them to visit back!
Make it as easy as possible for people to bookmark your page or subscribe you and consider reminding them to do so in the body of your content.

7. CLV (CUSTOMER LIFETIME VALUE)

Your CLV is your 'customer lifetime value'. This is the most important metric to track in terms of making money and it's another one you're going to have to calculate yourself by looking at a range of *other* metrics from your panel.

First, look at the amount you are charging for your product and more importantly how much you make for each sale. What is your profit margin for each unit you shift? This will be the RRP minus your 'COGs' (cost of goods sold). And while you're at it, don't forget to look at any discounts you might offer sometimes or the cost of delivery etc.

From here, you can then look at your number of unique visitors and the total number of sales. Roughly divide the total profit per year by the number of visitors and you have a rough average value for each of your customers.

Customer Lifetime Value really measures the value of *all* your leads and visits. In other words, buying customers are worth X amount of money to you and visitors who never buy from you are worth 0. But if you take the average amount, then you can work out a value for *each* visitor to your site, which we call CLV.

If you have 100 visitors, 1% conversion rates and a product worth $100 (with 100% profit) then each visitor is worth $1 to you, because statistically they are likely to earn you $1.

What's more, is that you can then look at how many of those sales are *repeat* customers and factor this in to work out how many of your customers actually buy multiple times and are thus worth $500 in reality. This gives you a more long-term idea of how much you can earn from a visitor, except it's worth noting that cash flow issues might rear their ugly head here.

To increase your customer lifetime value, you simply need to improve your conversion rates and your targeting. If you make your money from adverts meanwhile, then you could increase your CLV by looking at your AdSense optimization. How well placed are the adverts around your site? How relevant are the ads being shown?

What if you don't want to sell anything from your website? What if your aim is simply to build trust and gain a massive following?

Well in that case, you should *still* consider the CLV. This is still important because it is going to give you a budget for marketing your site and for promoting yourself. And this in turn will result in more hits.

It is up to you how you decide to define a 'customer' – whether that means a visitor, an email subscriber or an *actual* customer. And this will depend on your goals.

Which brings us nicely to the next metric…

8.   CPA, CPL AND ROI

CPA is the 'Cost Per Action' and this is a term that becomes relevant when you start paying for advertising.

If you use Google AdWords or Facebook Ads to try and drive more visitors to your website, then this is a form of PPC advertising. That stands for 'Pay Per Click' and it basically means that you're paying a certain amount for each person who clicks on your ad and thereby paying a certain amount for each new visitor.

PPC tells you how much you are spending and allows you to tightly control that number. But it tells you nothing of the value that you're getting in return. This will elevate your visits and that's all – you want to elevate your sales.

This is where 'CPA' comes in and uses goal tracking to show you how much you are spending for each person to buy a product from you. If you use Google Analytics and combine that with AdWords, then you can literally see how many of the clicks you get from your ad campaign are resulting in sales and this in turn allows you to work out the average amount you pay for each new sale.

Meanwhile, a 'CPL' is a 'Cost Per Lead', which tells you how much you are paying for leads. A lead will often be considered a warm lead who subscribes to your mailing list – but you could also choose to count highly engaged visitors as your warm leads. To calculate a CPL in this way, you could look at your number of visitors and then compare this to the average page views per visit or the average time on site. That way, you can work out the percentage of your visitors who end up being engaged visitors and therefore leads.

Of course you can also calculate your CPA and CPL without using Google Analytics or AdSense. If you are paying an SEO company to help your site to climb the SERPs for example, then you can calculate your CPA by looking at the amount you're spending on that marketing versus the number of sales and the amount of profit you are making. This is simply all your costs versus all of your profits.

Likewise, you can work this out if you sell through a mailing list by looking at how much you are paying for each lead who subscribes and then looking at the lifetime value of each subscribe. How many of them read your emails and how many of them buy your products?

How to Improve CPA and CPL

One way to improve your CPA and CPL is to target the right niche – one that isn't too competitive so that you can reduce the cost of advertising in that industry. Another is to make sure that you have done everything you can to reduce your bounce rates, improve engagement and enhance conversion rates so that the people you are paying to bring to your site are *actually* likely to buy from you. You can also do this by increasing the value of the product you sell, so that you improve the profit for each sale or by tweaking and improving your sales page to enhance conversions.

Another trick is to use advertising that charges on a CPA basis. Facebook now offers this service and allows you to set up CPA ads for things like page likes and even sales of special offers.
This way, you can agree to *only* pay when a click turns into a positive action – rather than wasting money on an ineffectual or poorly targeted campaign!

Oh and CPL is also improved by delivering an amazing product and excellent service of course! If people don't enjoy the experience of shopping with you, they won't do it again!

What to do With This Data

All this work is going to help you to calculate how much you are spending on the types of leads and customers you are aiming to bring to your site and how much you are earning from them.

If you pay for 100 clicks and each costs you $1 but you have a conversion rate of 1% and they pay $200, then your customer is worth $2 to you and you are only paying $1. If some customers tend to buy repeatedly, then your average value might be worth even more.

This then helps you to ensure that your final metric – your ROI – is high. Your ROI is your return on investment which tells you how much of the money you are spending on advertising, hosting and everything else you are getting back.

If your average customer is worth MORE to you than you are pay-ing to bring them to your website, then you can rest assured that you will not lose money and you will continue to reliably bring in profit that will increase over time.

By working out your customer lifetime value, you can work out what your budget is for advertising spend and that way keep growing and scaling your business while minimizing risk. Meanwhile, you can continue to improve your conversion rates and organic traffic in order to make more sales and allow yourself to spend more on those adverts.

By tracking *all* of this data and looking at it in a synergistic and cohesive manner, you can predict exactly your earnings, you can identify where to invest your money and you can look at the fail-ings that are damaging your profits and your engagement.

It takes time to get a handle on all this data but once you manage it, you can take the guesswork out of your internet marketing and turn it into a simple equation.

And the answer to that equation = success.

ABOUT THE AUTHOR

Charles Abeghe

Charles ABEGHE is a Canadian Entrepreneur, Golf, Wine and Music connoisseur based in Calgary, Alberta. Charles began his professional career as a Petroleum Engineer. He later received an MBA in International Business from the University of New Orleans, Louisiana, USA. He is a strong advocate of personal development for self improvement and financial independence.

He built a career spanning more than 20 years in the energy sector and worked in many countries including the USA, Canada, France, South Korea, Italy, UK, South Africa, Nigeria, Ghana, Liberia and Mali. He cares deeply about sustainable living, knowledge sharing, wealth & wellness, poverty alleviation and technology.

Charles's life has been guided by the Mantra "As A Man Thinketh" based on the book by the English Author – James Allen. This book was given to him by a teacher in the Catholic High school he had attended. The ideas and principles in this book provided a strong foundation for his character and belief system and is credited for propelling the child from a humble beginning to a life beyond his wildest expectations.

Charles enjoys sampling wine, collecting music from different parts of the world, golfing at his leisure time, knowledge sharing and continuous improvement. He further speaks many languages including English, French, Hausa, Ibo and Tiv. Charles is married to Irene with children.

www.ingramcontent.com/pod-product-compliance
Lightning Source LLC
Chambersburg PA
CBHW030547220526
45463CB00007B/3020